Little
Pebble™

Our Pets

Dogs

by Lisa J. Amstutz

D1372291

CAPSTONE PRESS
a capstone imprint

Little Pebble is published by Capstone Press,
1710 Roe Crest Drive, North Mankato, Minnesota 56003
www.mycapstone.com

Library of Congress Cataloging-in-Publication Data
Names: Amstutz, Lisa J., author.
Title: Dogs / by Lisa Amstutz.
Description: North Mankato, Minnesota : Capstone Press, [2018] | Series:
    Little pebble. Our pets | Audience: Ages 4–8. | Audience: K to grade 3.
Identifiers: LCCN 2017028021 (print) | LCCN 2017029773 (ebook) |
    ISBN 9781543501803 (eBook PDF) | ISBN 9781543501612 (hardcover) |
    ISBN 9781543501681 (paperback)
Subjects: LCSH: Dogs—Juvenile literature.
Classification: LCC SF426.5 (ebook) | LCC SF426.5 .A47 2018 (print) | DDC
    636.7—dc23
LC record available at https://lccn.loc.gov/2017028021

Editorial Credits
Marissa Kirkman, editor; Juliette Peters (cover) and Charmaine Whitman (interior), designers;
Morgan Walters, media researcher; Laura Manthe, production specialist

Image Credits
iStockphoto: JMichl, left 9; Shutterstock: Africa Studio, 21, alexei_tm, 5, anetapics, 13, Anna
Goroshnikova, 1, Anna Hoychuk, top right 9, 17, Dora Zett, back cover, frank60, 15, Grisha
Bruev, bottom 11, Kateryna Mostova, 7, Mr Aesthetics, (wood) design element throughout,
otsphoto, Cover, Richard Chaff, top 11, Yuriy Koronovskiy, 19

Printed and bound in the United States of America.
080819 002559

Table of Contents

Listen!

Woof!

What is that sound?

It is a dog barking!

This barking dog is excited.

It's time for a walk!

The dog wags its tail.

All About Dogs

Some dogs are big.

They can almost fill a bathtub.

Other dogs are tiny.

They can fit in your lap.

Look at those curls!

Dogs have all kinds of coats.

Some have long, soft hair.

Others have short, stiff hair.

Dogs have some
very good senses.
They hear sounds people can't.
Dogs can follow a scent trail.
Sniff!

Growing Up

Look!

A litter of puppies is born.

They drink milk from mom.

Puppies grow fast.
In four weeks, they
eat solid food.

Dogs and You

Dogs love to play
with you.
They can go get a ball.
Fetch!

Dogs are great friends.

They are loyal.

Dogs are happy just to be with you!

Glossary

coat—an animal's hair or fur

fetch—to go after something and bring it back; some dogs will fetch a ball or a toy

litter—a group of animals born at the same time to the same mother

loyal—being true to something or someone

puppy—a young dog

scent—a smell

sense—a way of knowing about your surroundings; hearing, smelling, touching, tasting, and sight are senses

sniff—to breathe in quickly through the nose

wag—to move from side to side; dogs wag their tails when they are happy

Read More

Graubart, Norman D. *My Dog.* Pets Are Awesome!
New York: PowerKids Press, 2014.

Shores, Erika L. *Pet Dogs Up Close.* Pets Up Close.
North Mankato, Minn.: Capstone Press, 2015.

Stoltman, Joan. *My First Dog.* Let's Get a Pet!
New York: Gareth Stevens Publishing, 2017.

Internet Sites

Use FactHound to find Internet sites
related to this book.

Visit www.facthound.com

Just type in 9781543501612 and go.

Check out projects, games and lots more at
www.capstonekids.com

Critical Thinking Questions

1. Would you like to own a dog? Why or why not?

2. What do newborn puppies eat?

3. Why do dogs make good pets?

Index